Storïau Cyn

Y RHIA
GWSG

Lluniau gan Stephen Cartwright

Cymraeg gan Roger Boore

Chwiliwch am yr hwyaden fâch felen ar bob tudalen.

Un tro, roedd 'na Frenin a Brenhines oedd yn drist
iawn am nad oedd ganddynt blant. Yna, ar ôl
blynyddoedd lawer, ganed merch fach iddynt.
Roeddent wrth eu bodd, ac yn caru'r baban yn fawr
iawn.

Adeg bedyddio'r Dywysoges fach, trefnodd y Brenin
wledd fawr yn y Palas. Gwahoddodd chwech o
dylwythod da, ond anghofiodd wahodd un dylwythen
ddrwg nad oedd neb wedi'i gweld ers hydoedd.
Roedd honno'n ddig ofnadwy.

Wedi'r wledd, gwnaeth y tylwythod da ddymuniadau dros y baban. Dymunasant iddi fod yn hardd, yn raslon, yn ddeallus, ac yn un dda am ganu a dawnsio. Ond cyn i'r chweched dylwythen ddymuno, daeth y dylwythen ddrwg i mewn.

"Dyma fy nymuniad i i'r baban," meddai hi. "Yn ddwy ar bymtheg oed, bydd hi'n pigo ei bys ar dröell, ac yn marw."

"Na'n wir!" ebe'r chweched dylwythen. "Yn lle marw, rwy'n dymuno iddi gysgu am gan mlynedd."

Yna diflannodd y dylwythen ddrwg mewn cwmwl o
fwg. "Iawn," meddai'r Brenin, "fe wna i ddeddf
newydd. Rhaid i bob tröell yn y deyrnas gael ei llosgi.
Wedyn wnaiff y Dywysoges ddim pigo'i bys."

Tyfodd y Dywysoges i fod yn hardd, yn raslon, yn
ddeallus, ac yn un dda am ganu a dawnsio. Ar ei
phen-blwydd yn ddwy ar bymtheg oed, bu Dawns
Fawr yn y Palas, a daeth y tylwythod da. Chofiodd neb
am y dylwythen ddrwg.

Drannoeth, wrth grwydro'r Palas, daeth y Dywysoges ar draws stafell ddieithr.

Yn y stafell gwelai hen wraig a chanddi dröell. "Tyrd i mewn, 'merch i," ebe honno. Y dylwythen ddrwg oedd hi.

"Beth ŷch chi'n 'wneud?" holodd y Dywysoges, oedd heb weld tröell o'r blaen. "Nyddu," meddai'r hen wraig. "Wyt ti eisiau trio? Tyrd, dal hwn." Estynnodd y Dywysoges ei llaw. "Ow!" meddai. "Rwy wedi pigo fy mys."

Mewn chwinciad, syrthiodd y Dywysoges i gysgu.
Syrthiodd y Brenin a'r Frenhines a phawb arall yn y
Palas i gysgu hefyd.

Aeth y chwe thylwythen dda â'r Dywysoges gwsg i'w
stafell a'i dodi ar y gwely.

Yn y Palas ni symudodd yr un creadur byw am gan mlynedd. Tyfodd coedwig drwchus o'i gwmpas, gan guddio popeth ond y to. Aeth neb ar gyfyl y Palas ond y chwe thylwythen dda, a fu'n gwarchod tra bod pawb yn cysgu.

Ymhen union gan mlynedd, roedd Tywysog ifanc yn hela ger y goedwig. Gwelodd do'r Palas, a holodd ei hanes i hen ŵr. "Dwedodd fy nhaid mai palas swyn yw e," meddai'r hen ŵr, "a bod tywysoges hardd yn cysgu ynddo."

"Diolch," meddai'r Tywysog, a dechrau cerdded tua'r Palas. Symudodd y coed o'r neilltu gan agor llwybr iddo.

Rhedodd i fyny grisiau'r Palas, heibio i'r milwyr cwsg. Roedd popeth yn gwbl dawel.

Chwiliodd trwy'r Palas i gyd, nes cyrraedd stafell y
Dywysoges. Roedd hi mor hardd fel y plygodd ef
drosti a'i chusanu. Agorodd y Dywysoges ei llygaid gan
wenu. "Dyma ti wedi dod o'r diwedd," meddai hi.

Ymhob rhan o'r Palas roedd pobl yn dihuno, yn dylyfu gên, ac yn ysgwyd llwch ymaith. "Heno fe gawn ni wledd," meddai'r Brenin. Diolchodd i'r Tywysog am eu hachub, a gwahoddodd y Frenhines ef i'r wledd.

Drannoeth, gofynnodd y Tywysog i'r Brenin a gâi
briodi'r Dywysoges. "Cei, wrth gwrs," meddai'r Brenin.
Bu priodas fawr, a'r chwe thylwythen yno hefyd. A bu
fyw'r Tywysog a'r Dywysoges yn llawen byth wedyn.

© Usborne Publishing Ltd 1988
© y fersiwn Gymraeg Gwasg y Dref Wen 1989
Cyhoeddwyd gan Wasg y Dref Wen, 28 Ffordd yr Eglwys, Yr Eglwys Newydd, Caerdydd.
Argraffwyd ym Mhortiwgal. Cedwir pob hawlfraint.

Lana Spinks

Winter

Nightingale Books

A CIP catalogue record for this title is available from the British Library.
ISBN 978-1-83875-506-5

Nightingale Books is an imprint of
Pegasus Elliot MacKenzie Publishers Ltd.
www.pegasuspublishers.com

First Published in 2023

Nightingale Books
Sheraton House Castle Park
Cambridge England

Printed & Bound in Great Britain

Dedication

This book is dedicated to my granddaughters,

Winter and Olive.

Winter, Spring, Summer and Autumn are four sisters who live in their own houses in a place called The Dengie.

Winter has a house near a park and lives with her pet rabbit, Dit. He is a small black rabbit with a fluffy tail, a pink nose, very long grey whiskers and short ears. Winter has curly blonde hair and bright blue eyes. Winter loves the snow, and her favourite activity is playing in it. This is a story about Winter and Dit on a snowy day.

Winter was fast asleep, all cosy and warm, in her comfortable bed. The sun was shining brightly through her window, and she could have happily stayed there all day except for one thing. Dit was hungry! So, Dit was tickling her face with his long whiskers to get her attention! Winter slowly opened her eyes. "Morning, Dit! I know, you want your breakfast, don't you? Come on then, I will get up now."

Dit hopped off the bed as Winter sat up, rubbing her eyes and yawning loudly. "I wonder what sort of day it is?" she said to Dit as she clambered over to look out from her bedroom window.

"Wow, Dit! It has been snowing!"

Winter ran down the stairs and flung open the front door, just to make sure. "Yep, still snowing!"

Winter shut the door and put on her warm blue coat and matching hat over her pyjamas. Turning to look for her wellington boots, she heard, "Thump! Thump! Thump!"

It was Dit! Drawing her attention to his empty bowl! He was sitting waiting for his breakfast. "I am sorry, Dit. I will get your breakfast right now!" she laughed. Winter took off her coat and hat and found Dit a large juicy carrot in the cupboard.

Winter left Dit munching happily while she ate her breakfast of creamy porridge and drank a cup of warm sweet tea, and then went upstairs to get out of her pyjamas, make her bed and clean her teeth.

Once she had washed and was dressed in her warmest clothes, she was so excited at the thought of a whole day filled with fun in the snow. When she came back downstairs, Winter found Dit fast asleep on his blanket by the fire.

She put on her blue coat with its matching hat, pulled on her wellington boots over her thick blue socks, and finally wrapped a long blue scarf around her neck. "That should certainly keep me warm enough!"

"Now, where is my sledge?" Winter said to herself.

"I remember! I'm sure it's at the back of the shed! I'm off now, Dit," she called out to him. "Are you sure you don't want to come with me?"

Dit raised his head and slowly hid under his blanket with just his nose poking out.

"Well, I'll be down the park if you change your mind. See ya!"

Winter opened her front door, found the sledge in the shed, and made her way to the park, pulling her sledge behind her.

The snow was very thick and made a crunching sound as Winter walked along the path towards the park.

Then, suddenly out of nowhere, a snowball flew through the air and landed with a dull "Thud!" hitting Winter on the back of her coat and making her jump!

"Hey! who did that?" shouted Winter crossly.

"Sorry, Winter! It was me." a voice sang out from behind the slides.

Winter turned around and saw a little girl with bright red hair and a bright red coat, hat and gloves to match. It was her sister, Autumn!

"Where are you off to?" demanded Autumn.

"To the hill on the other side of the park," Winter replied. "I think it will be perfect for sledging with all the snow." Then, she added excitedly, "do you want to come with me?"

"OK", replied Autumn.

The two girls chatted happily as they walked along, and when they finally reached the hilltop, they prepared the sledge for take-off! Autumn sat at the front, holding on to the pull cord, her legs pointing out to help with the steering. Winter crouched at the back, holding firmly to each side of the sledge. "Ready? Here we go!" Winter yelled as she ran a few steps and gave one last great shove before jumping on the back... "Wheeeee!" Both girls screamed at the top of their voices as they sped down the slope.

"Wow, that's such fun! I want to do it again!" shouted Autumn when they reached the end of the slope.

So they did. They climbed the hill again, jumped on the sledge and "Wheeeee!" Once more, down they sped. Time and again, they repeated the fun, taking turns to steer and push. After a while, Winter decided she wanted to do something else.

"Let's make a snowman," said Winter.

"How do you make a snowman?" asked Autumn.

"Everyone knows how to make a snowman!" said Winter rolling her eyes.

"Well, I don't." said Autumn shrugging her shoulders.

"I'll help you." said Winter. "First of all, you make a snowball in your hand, then you keep adding snow and rolling it around, and when it is too big for your hands, roll it on the ground. Gradually it will get bigger and bigger" she explained...

So that is what they did. First, they made a big ball for the body, then a slightly smaller ball for the head.

When they had lifted the head onto the body, they stood back to review their work.

"Now we need to find something to make the arms." said Winter searching around the ground.

"What about these two long twigs?" suggested Autumn.

"Perfect!" said Winter.

Autumn found some old conkers in her pocket and used them to make the eyes and mouth.

"He needs a nose!" said Winter.

"But what can we use for that?" asked Autumn.

"I know the perfect thing!" Winter exclaimed. "Wait here, and I'll be back as soon as I can."

Winter ran all the way back home. She opened the front door really quietly, took off her boots and crept through the hall into the kitchen. Her plan was not to disturb Dit, who was sleeping peacefully. She opened the cupboard, and there on the shelf sat... his very last carrot! Quickly she stuffed it into her pocket. Winter crept past Dit back into the hall, then pulled her boots on again, and quietly opened the front door.

She ran all the way back to the park where Autumn was waiting. Winter took the carrot from her pocket and placed it on the face of the snowman.

"There! All finished," said Winter.

The girls looked at the snowman for a while, admiring their hard work, and then they played in the snow until it began to get dark, and it started to snow again.

"We should go home. It's getting really cold," said Autumn.

"OK, I'll see you later," said Winter, giving her sister a hug and waving as she pulled her sledge towards home.

On the way home, Winter stopped at the local farm shop to buy a bunch of fresh juicy carrots for Dit.

When she had put her sledge back in the shed and put her coat, hat, gloves and wellington boots in the cupboard to dry, she went into the kitchen. She found Dit still sleeping peacefully, all cosy and warm in his blanket by the fire, probably dreaming about carrots!

At the sound of Winter, he opened his eyes, yawned and then hopped over to his bowl looking into it expectantly. "Here you are, Dit! I used your last carrot to make a nose for a snowman, but I have bought a whole bunch of fresh carrots for your tea."

This news made Dit very happy. While he was eating, Winter told him all about the wonderful day with Autumn in the park and how they had both enjoyed playing together in the snow.

About the Author

Lana was born in Colchester in 1970, where she lived with her family. As a child Lana loved telling stories to her friends. In 1991 she married her husband Andrew and later moved to Burnham on Crouch with their two children.

Lana worked in a primary school for 13 years.

After her granddaughters were born, Lana wrote the story of Winter, which came about from a dream.

Acknowledgements

Many thanks to my family and friends,

especially Siobhan Gower.